CELEBRATING THE FAMILY NAME OF HAWKINS

Celebrating the Family Name of Hawkins

Walter the Educator

Silent King Books
a WhichHead Entertainment Imprint

Copyright © 2024 by Walter the Educator

All rights reserved. No part of this book may be reproduced in any manner whatsoever without written permission except in the case of brief quotations embodied in critical articles and reviews.

First Printing, 2024

Disclaimer

This book is a literary work; the story is not about specific persons, locations, situations, and/or circumstances unless mentioned in a historical context. Any resemblance to real persons, locations, situations, and/or circumstances is coincidental. This book is for entertainment and informational purposes only. The author and publisher offer this information without warranties expressed or implied. No matter the grounds, neither the author nor the publisher will be accountable for any losses, injuries, or other damages caused by the reader's use of this book. The use of this book acknowledges an understanding and acceptance of this disclaimer.

Celebrating the Family Name of Hawkins is a memory book that belongs to the Celebrating Family Name Book Series by Walter the Educator. Collect them all and more books at WaltertheEducator.com

USE THE EXTRA SPACE TO DOCUMENT YOUR FAMILY MEMORIES THROUGHOUT THE YEARS

HAWKINS

The name of Hawkins, strong and proud,

A heritage that speaks aloud.

From rolling hills to cities bright,

Their mark is cast in morning light.

Through time's long thread, they journeyed far,

With dreams as high as the northern star.

In fields they tilled, in waves they sailed,

Their spirits bold, their hearts unveiled.

With laughter rich and stories deep,

The Hawkins' tales are ones to keep.

They gather close, in warmth they stand,

A woven quilt, a close-knit band.

From rugged roots and boundless grace,

They've built a legacy, a place.

Through trials met and mountains climbed,

They forge ahead, both true and kind.

A name that carries strength in song,

The Hawkins bond is fierce and strong.

In every heart, a fire burns,

A light that lives as seasons turn.

They honor past, they cherish now,

With steadfast gaze, they make a vow.

To hold the torch of those who came,

And bear with pride the Hawkins name.

Inventors, thinkers, artists, guides,

With wisdom that in each resides.

They craft their path, they blaze their trail,

With steady hands, they never fail.

In fields of green, on shores of sand,

They leave their touch, their hopeful hand.

Through generations, young and old,

The Hawkins story shines like gold.

From laughter's ring in summer's sun,

To fireside tales when day is done,

They weave a bond both rich and rare,

A tapestry of love and care.

In every dawn, in twilight's hue,

The Hawkins spirit rises new.

With open hearts and courage fierce,

They seek the world, its depths to pierce.

ABOUT THE CREATOR

Walter the Educator is one of the pseudonyms for Walter Anderson. Formally educated in Chemistry, Business, and Education, he is an educator, an author, a diverse entrepreneur, and he is the son of a disabled war veteran. "Walter the Educator" shares his time between educating and creating. He holds interests and owns several creative projects that entertain, enlighten, enhance, and educate, hoping to inspire and motivate you. Follow, find new works, and stay up to date with Walter the Educator™

at WaltertheEducator.com

Milton Keynes UK
Ingram Content Group UK Ltd.
UKHW022051111124
451035UK00014B/1063